CW00519356

ISBN: 979-83-771-2669-0

Print on demand by Amazon

Table of contents

Introduction

The concept of reselling is a simple and effective way to make money. Reselling is a term that characterizes the act of reselling a product that you have purchased or own in order to make a profit. However, it is essential to understand how reselling works in order to succeed in this business. It is possible to generate a supplemental income or even make a living in this field if you invest enough time and effort and are determined to succeed.

This book contains tips, advice and illustrated techniques that will allow you to buy at the best price and sell at the price you want. We will explore in depth the different aspects of reselling on Vinted. We'll cover topics such as which products and brands to buy and resell, how to spot and get started with niche products, how to create effective ads, and tips for maximizing your profits. We will also look at different strategies and tools to find products at a good price and how to sell them at a higher price. In short, I will give you all the tips you need to make money with reselling on Vinted.

PART 1: Trends and brands to know for reselling products on Vinted

Identify current market trends and popular brands

When you are in the business of buying and reselling, you need to choose the items you buy wisely. Many products can be resold at a profit, such as clothing, jewelry, video games or even books.

In order to buy the best items at the right price, it is important to know the current trends and to anticipate those that are likely to develop in the market. It is also necessary to analyze the sales of other users to get an idea of which products are selling best.

One of the current trends in the resale market on Vinted is the increased demand for vintage branded clothing. Buyers are looking for unique and timeless pieces from the 80s and 90s, such as denim shirts, hoodies and leather jackets. Brands like Tommy Hilfiger, Ralph Lauren and Levi's are particularly popular in this category.

Ethical and sustainable fashion has also become a growing trend on Vinted. Shoppers are looking for clothing made from eco-friendly and ethical materials, such as organic cotton and linen, and brands that embrace sustainable production practices. Brands like Patagonia, Eileen Fisher and Stella McCartney are popular in this category.

Streetwear is also in high demand on Vinted. Brands like Supreme, Off-White and Adidas Yeezy attract shoppers looking for fashionable and exclusive pieces. The most sought-after pieces include t-shirts, hoodies and sneakers.

Finally, luxury brands remain popular on Vinted. Shoppers are looking for branded pieces like Gucci, Louis Vuitton and Chanel. Handbags, shoes and accessories are particularly in demand.

When starting out, I would advise you to start small and focus on brand name items that are guaranteed to be resold. For clothing, you should choose the most popular brands such as Nike, Adidas, Ralph Lauren, Carhartt, Lacoste, Levi's, The North Face, Patagonia, Moncler and Tommy Hilfiger. It is also possible to focus on luxury brands like Louis Vuitton, Gucci, Chanel, Dior or Prada.

Vinted's value-added products

- Branded clothing (Nike, Adidas, Ralph Lauren, Lacoste, Levi's, Carhartt, Patagonia, Moncler)
- Luxury clothing (Louis Vuitton, Gucci, Chanel, Balenciaga, Dior, Hermès, Burberry)
- Soccer team jerseys (Paris Saint-Germain, Juventus, Liverpool, Barcelona, Real Madrid)
- Sports shoes (Jordan, Nike Dunk, Air Force 1)
- Trading cards (Pokémon, Panini)
- Branded perfumes and cosmetics (Dior, Chanel, Guerlain)
- Jewelry (Pandora)
- Rare books or comics (old Tintin comics)
- Video games and consoles (PS5, Nintendo Switch, Nintendo DS)
- Toys (Lego, Playmobil)
- Figurines and dolls (Barbie, Disney, Harry Potter, Funko Pop)
- Collectors' items (Vinyl, old objects)
- Valuable items more or less old (GameBoy DMG-01, Nokia 3310)

Please note that this list is not exhaustive. There are many other products that can be successfully resold on Vinted. It will be necessary to continue to explore new options and to constantly adapt to the evolution of market trends.

PART 2: Analysis of an ad and the seller profile

Analyzing the ad and the seller's profile is the first thing to check before buying an item.

Verify the authenticity and condition of the items

Analyzing the ads on Vinted is the key to a successful resale. It is important to look at the pictures carefully because some sellers may not point out defects in the description but show them in the pictures. Sellers can add up to 20 images per listing, so it's helpful to review them carefully to avoid unpleasant surprises.

Be sure to check the item carefully for any stains, snags, scratches, wear and tear, or defects. Check that the photos were taken by the seller, as this will ensure that you are buying an authentic item. Use this information to evaluate the product and make an informed decision about the purchase.

With the growing popularity of Vinted, take precautions to avoid scams when purchasing. Unfortunately, fake accounts and products are very common on this platform. To avoid falling into these traps, here are some tips to assess the honesty of sellers.

Avoiding scams

To minimize scams, look at the number of reviews on the seller's profile. A seller who will have more than 50 5-star reviews is generally considered trustworthy. However, be careful if the seller has less than 10 5-star reviews. Some sellers may conduct fake transactions to get positive reviews and continue selling fakes. So check to see if the transactions that led to those positive reviews are recent. If all sales are less than a month old, beware.

The information available on the seller's profile should be taken into account when purchasing on Vinted. In addition to the photo and description, check the city of residence, the date of the last login and the number of subscribers. This can give you an idea of the experience and reliability of the seller.

It is also important to check the seller's ratings. If they average less than 5 stars, check the reviews to understand why. If the seller lives near you, you can also consider hand delivery for large or contentious purchases. However, be careful with this method as it will not allow you to benefit from the buyer-seller protection.

A last connection date that is several weeks old may indicate that the seller is not present and that your product may take some time to be shipped, if at all. So be wary before placing an order.

You should take into account the interest indicators of other Vinted users when considering purchasing an item on the platform. On the product page, you can measure the interest of other users using the number of views and favorites. An item with a high number of views is generally considered popular. Also, when an item has several favorites, you should act quickly so as not to miss the opportunity.

Don't hesitate to ask the seller for more details about the item you are coveting. You can ask for measurements of the item, photos of worn items or more specific photos of the reported defect. For example, ask the seller to send you photos of areas that are described as damaged in the item description.

This is also an opportunity to see if the seller is receptive and willing to sell the item. You can negotiate a more reasonable price.

By following these tips, you can shop safely on Vinted. But it is important to remember that even with all the necessary precautions, there is always a risk of fraud. So be vigilant and use common sense when shopping.

PART 3: Items to maximize your resale profits

Branded clothing

As we have seen before, popular brands will be preferred. Neutral colors such as black, gray or white are often more sought after as they can be combined with many different styles and appeal to a wider range of people. Bright colors and prints can be a harder sell because they are often associated with more specific styles.

Also, it's best to focus on the most in-demand sizes, such as S, M and L, which are the easiest to resell. Extreme sizes, such as XS or XL, can be more difficult to sell as they are less common and may not fit everyone.

The following pages give you a selection of popular garments with indicative purchase and resale price targets to start your first clothing resell.

Nike Jogging

Purchase price: between 15 and 20 €

Resale price: between 30 and 35 €

Ralph Lauren hoodie

Purchase price: between 50 and 60 €

Resale price: between 80 and 100 €

Lacoste hoodie

Purchase price: between 30 and 40 €

Resale price: between 60 and 70 €

The North Face 700 Nuptse Jacket

Purchase price: between 100 and 120 €

Resale price: between 170 and 200 €

Lacoste sweater

Purchase price: between 30 and 40 €

Resale price: between 60 and 70 €

Nike Sweater

Purchase price: between 20 and 25 €

Resale price: between 30 and 45 €

Moncler Maya down jacket

Purchase price: between 200 and 300 €

Resale price: between 500 and 600 €

Patagonia fleece

Purchase price: between 70 and 80 €

Resale price: between 120 and 130 €

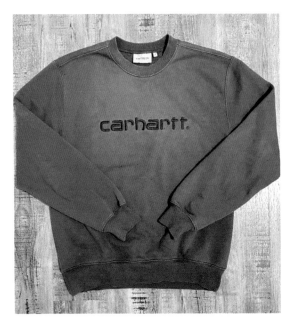

Carhartt sweatshirt

Purchase price: between 30 and 40 €

Resale price: between 60 and 70 €

Negotiate the price

Dare to negotiate the price of the items you want, only if the offer is strong and competitive. Indeed, negotiation is only effective for items that do not sell quickly. With a large amount of traffic on the site, the most popular items can go very quickly and there will be no room for negotiation. However, if an ad hasn't received any bids in over a week or there are many other similar ads available, it is possible to negotiate the price.

By using this strategy, you could save several hundred dollars on your purchases. Keep in mind that it is possible to make an offer up to 40% cheaper than the base price. For example, if an item is listed at 100 euros, you could make an offer of 60 euros. Vinted offers you the possibility to send five offers per day.

Note that this offer is not binding on the buyer. Even if the offer is accepted, you still have the option of confirming or rejecting the transaction. The seller can also refuse the offer or make a counter-offer. It is common to reach a compromise after a few exchanges of offers.

Sellers may also offer to buy in batches to save on shipping costs. Depending on the number of items purchased, the discount can range from -5% to -50% on the package price.

20 niche products to maximize your profits

Reselling on Vinted is an effective way to make money, but to be successful it is important to find rare and in-demand products. These niches can be exploited to buy products at fair prices and resell them at higher prices, creating a scarcity for certain in-demand items.

Generally speaking, to find a niche, target out-of-print, high-demand products. That way, you will either have people who can afford them or who are passionate about them. Also, be aware that a good niche product sells out quickly on Vinted so you'll want to be the first to buy it.

Here are 20 niche products that I suggest that can be resold at a high price. In my case, I made real gains with the 1989 GameBoy DMG-01 by buying the GameBoy in its original box on one side and the Pokemon games in their original box on the other. I resold the whole set as a complete pack. If you manage to buy these products with their instructions, the value will be even higher when resold. Beware of scams and counterfeiting for Nintendo products. Old Nokia 3310 phones or other old comics (Tintin editions from 1943) are also part of my niche products. You can also turn to the Pop figurines which can be rare and whose prices keep increasing. Check out the specialized sites to find the rarest figurines. Finally, you will find my niche clothing with brands like Off-White, Stone Island, CP Compagny, Palm Angels, Corteiz, Yves Saint Laurent, Amis Paris, Dickies, Jacquemus, Maison Mihara Yasuhiro or Axel Arigato. These brands can be found on other products than those presented here.

GameBoy DMG-01 from 1989

Purchase price: between 50 and 60 €

Resale price: between 80 and 100 €

Pokémon blue, yellow and red cartridge

Purchase price: between 20 and 30 €

Resale price: between 50 and 60 €

Nokia 3310 in its original box

Purchase price: between 100 and 120 €

Resale price: between 150 and 180 €

Indiana Jones Pop Figure

Purchase price: between 70 and 80 €

Resale price: between 100 and 120 €

Tintin album

Purchase price: between 400 and 500 €

Resale price: between 2000 and 3500 €

Off-White Cut off hoodie

Purchase price: between 150 and 170 €

Resale price: between 200 and 220 €

Stone Island hoodie

Purchase price: between 80 and 130 €

Resale price: between 180 and 200 €

Hoodie CP Compagny

Purchase price: between 100 and 130 €

Resale price: between 200 and 230 €

Palm Angels hoodie

Purchase price: between 100 and 150 €

Resale price: between 200 and 250 €

Corteiz hoodie

Purchase price: between 70 and 100 €

Resale price: between 130 and 150 €

Canada Goose down jacket

Purchase price: between 300 and 400 €

Resale price: between 600 and 630 €

Yves Saint Laurent hoodie

Purchase price: between 150 and 200 €

Resale price: between 350 and 300 €

Palm Angels T-shirt

Purchase price: between 60 and 70 €

Resale price: between 90 and 120 €

Ami Paris sweater

Purchase price: between 80 and 90 €

Resale price: between 120 and 130 €

Dickies 874 pants

Purchase price: between 25 and 30 €

Resale price: between 40 and 50 €

Bob Jacquemus

Purchase price: between 70 and 80 €

Resale price: between 100 and 110 €

Maison Mihara Yasuhiro "Peterson" shoes

Purchase price: between 250 and 300 €

Resale price: between 400 and 430 €

New Balance 550 shoes

Purchase price: between 70 and 90 €

Resale price: between 130 and 150 €

Axel Arigato T-shirt

Purchase price: between 20 and 25 €

Resale price: between 30 and 40 €

Axel Arigato hoodie

Purchase price: between 50 and 60 €

Resale price: between 70 and 80 €

Find a niche

In your turn, I propose you to find your own niche product and earn money with it. Locate a retrogaming, vintage or rare product (clothing, sneakers, comics, Sega or Nintendo consoles, limited edition or discontinued items) and bookmark the item you find on Vinted. After you have bookmarked as many items in that niche as possible, check your Vinted notifications to see if the items have sold out. The most important thing will be to see at what price because selling is good but making a profit is better. Once you have determined that this product is a niche, buy it back at a lower price using a bot to make sure you don't miss out (see appendix). Resell it by taking your margin. That's it, you now have your niche!

Another tip is to anticipate trends with Google Trends which is a useful tool for anyone who wants to predict search trends on the web. You can view search trends on Google based on various criteria such as keyword, location and date. Use this tool to predict search trends on Vinted and discover more niche items and brands.

For example, if you search for the keyword "sweater" associated with the Paris region, you can see that the search trend for this item peaks in December of each year. This could indicate that shoppers are looking for sweaters in December (which is not illogical in itself).

For example, if you search for the keyword "sweater" associated with the Paris region, you can see that the search trend for this item peaks in December of each year. This could indicate that shoppers are looking for sweaters in December (which is not illogical in itself).

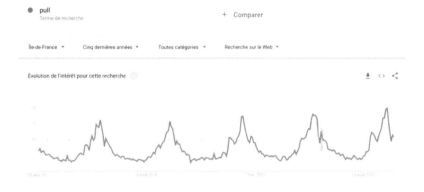

The column "Related queries" shows brands related to the keyword "pullover", such as Palm Angels, Ami Paris or Off-White. The keyword "pull plaid" was also found, which may indicate an interest in this type of sweater.

By switching from the "last five years" to the "last 12 months" time scale, we can observe that the associated queries are not the same and this can help us to refocus on the more recent or even current trend in the "last seven days" scale.

Requêtes associées ⑦	En progression ▼ ⬇ ⟨⟩ ⤳	
1 pull tommy hilfiger homme galeries lafayette		Record
2 sous pull kipsta		+5 000 %
3 pull tommy hilfiger galeries lafayette		+850 %
4 pull ralph lauren galeries lafayette		+650 %
5 pull stussy		+650 %

⟨ Affichage des requêtes 1 à 5 sur 25 ⟩

This information available on Google Trends allows sellers to anticipate search trends and highlight items and brands that are likely to catch buyers' attention.

PART 4: How to sell effectively on Vinted

Once you have purchased your items, you need to think about reselling them. In this part, I give you all the keys to succeed in your sale by posting a quality ad that will make you stand out from other sellers.

Fill in your profile

Before posting any ads, you must complete your biography on your account. As we have seen before, potential buyers will visit your profile page to determine if you are a trustworthy seller.

So to sell items on Vinted, it is essential to have a complete profile. This may seem obvious, but many sellers overlook this aspect. A complete profile usually includes a profile picture, a detailed biography and information about the terms of sale. First of all, make sure your profile name is short and preferably professional sounding (related to the type of products you will be selling). For example, choose "Sneakers_shop" or "Retrogaming_store" rather than "Sneakers01574" or "Retrogaming36". Profile pictures give a first impression to a potential buyer and show that the account is active. Your bio is also important, as it shows who you are, your shipping and selling terms, and your measurements. A complete profile gives buyers confidence that there is someone behind the account and that they are not buying from just anyone. This can also help increase sales, as buyers may feel more comfortable making an offer or asking questions about an item if they know who they are talking to.

These profiles are examples that may inspire you:

The importance of pictures

It is obvious that beauty attracts attention. That's why it is necessary to take care of the presentation of your ads to increase your chances of selling. But how do you create visually appealing ads? You don't need to be a photography expert to do this, just follow these simple steps:

- Use a quality camera or a good smartphone to take your photos

- Choose a plain background with elegant colors, such as a wooden floor, a table or tiles

- Add a warm glow to give your images depth

- Place your items on the solid background and make sure they are well lit

- Take photos in portrait or landscape format, but make sure they are not blurry

- Center your images and add light filters if you wish

By following these steps, you'll get stylish photos that will catch the attention of potential buyers. You can also add small colorful objects to your photo to make it original but keep it simple.

Here are some examples of attractive photos for a listing:

40,99 € ♡10
43,74 € incl. ⊘
L
Nike   Boosté

45,00 € ♡8
47,95 € incl. ⊘
S
Nike   Boosté

40,00 € ♡6
42,70 € incl. ⊘
L
Nike   Boosté

37,00 € ♡16
39,55 € incl. ⊘
L
Nike   Boosté

104,90 € ♡28
110,85 € incl. ⊘

Nintendo

1350,00 € ♡41
1418,20 € incl. ⊘

Louis Vuitton

Now that you have taken beautiful pictures, keep in mind that the description is also essential for the buyer.

Write beautiful ads

When selling your items on Vinted, the goal is to get the buyer to click the "buy" button. To do this, it is important to describe all the details of the item, provide information about its composition and size, and understand what it looks like.

First of all, you need to give as many details as possible about the item, such as different colors, buttons, zippers, lace inserts, mother of pearl buttons... This helps to clarify the look of the item and helps the buyer to make a decision. It is also important to provide information on the composition of the garment (cotton, wool, synthetic...). Buyers know what they are buying.

Also provide information on the size of the item and whether it fits small or large. This ensures that the buyer is ordering the right size. Also describe the fit of the item (narrow, straight, slim...) to understand how it fits the body and its look (what it could be worn with).

Finally, mention any small imperfections in the item if there are any (take pictures to avoid confusion for the buyer) and specify if the item is new, like new or barely worn. This will help unlock sales.

At the end of the description, in order for your items to show up in search results, add #'s at the end of the description (example: #winter #warm #black #doudoune #nike).

Once you've taken the photos and written the product description, you'll need to think carefully about the selling price you'll set, which will be an important factor in the purchase decision.

Here are some examples of descriptions that include the elements we have seen for a good description:

Sweat/Pull Adidas noir

- Sweat / Pull Adidas noir
- Taille M
- Très bon état (Cordon manquant !)
- 5% pour les abonnés
- N'hésitez pas à m'envoyer un message si vous avez une question
- Envoi rapide et sécurisé

#sweatadidas #pulladidas #hoodieadidas
#sweatshirtadidas #survêtement #adidas
#sportswear #adidasoriginals
#vintage #y2k #vintageluxe #luxe #luxury
#brand #fashion #mode #streetwear
#veste #mixte

Pull Nike Marron Clair

- | Négociable uniquement avec les abonné(e)s
- | Pull Nike
- | Marron Clair
- | Référence : BV2654-258
- | État : Très bon état
- | 80% Coton / 20% Polyester
- | Taille S, dimensions détaillées :
- Longueur du sweat : 63CM
- Longueur des manches : 57CM
- Largeur d'aisselle à aisselle : 52CM
- | J'expédie mes colis le jour de l'achat ou le lendemain (hors période week-end)
- | Pour toutes questions, n'hésitez pas à m'envoyer un message

— — — — — — — — — — — — — —
— — — — —

#Nike #Jogging #Sport #Homme
#Survetement #Ensemble #Pull
#Sweat #marseille #vintedgift

Sweat nike vintage| ⊙

Sweat nike bleu
Taille xl (mais taille comme un L)
aucuns défauts
Envoi rapide
Lavage avant envoi

#streetwear #nike #blue # sweat
#pull #style #vintage #nikevin-
tage

Pricing to maximize your chances of selling

When setting the price, remember that you are selling mainly
second-hand items, so there is no need to be too greedy (unless
it is a niche, rare, old, sought-after or no longer produced
item). In general, analyze the prices set by other sellers on the
same type of item you are going to sell. I advise you to set the
price slightly lower than the others if you want to sell quickly.

On the other hand, if you are not in a hurry to sell, you can
match the competition or even set a price slightly higher than
the others if your item is in very good condition. You can
always modify the ad later to lower the price if your item does
not sell. Moreover, if potential buyers had bookmarked your
item and were therefore interested, a notification will be sent
to them when your item drops. You can potentially close the
sale at that time.

Selling seasonal items

Buyers are generally looking for seasonal clothing or products. Therefore, follow the year's calendar to make your sales as successful as possible. Swimsuits will have to wait until next spring-summer while the sale of down jackets will be favored during the winter.

Nevertheless, buying items that are not in season can be an asset to better resell them later (with a capital gain). Indeed, you can always negotiate the price with the seller since few people will be interested in a swimsuit during the winter. Fill your inventory during the winter and bring it out in the spring-summer to maximize your profits.

Choose the time of uploading

To increase your visibility on Vinted, it is important to choose the best time to post your ad. Users tend to log on more frequently at certain times of the day and on certain days of the week. Therefore, it is important to know these times to improve the chances of your ad being seen.

The best days of the week to post are generally Tuesday, Thursday, Saturday and Sunday. Days with significant temperature changes are also good days to post an ad, as this can encourage consumers to look for clothing that can handle these changes. The evening, from 9:00 to 10:30 p.m. is also a good time to post an ad, as this is usually when Vinted users have the most time to browse the site.

Another thing to consider is the time of the month you post your ad. The beginning of the month is usually the time when consumers are most likely to make a purchase, as they have just received their paychecks. Therefore, it is advisable to place an ad at this time to maximize the chances of making a sale.

Conclusion

In summary, the key to successful reselling on Vinted is to look for rare and high-demand products, coupled with monitoring offers and good buying strategies. Constantly continue to identify market trends and popular brands that will allow you to buy at the best price and resell at a higher price.

Analyzing the ads and the seller's authenticity will help guide your choices and avoid scams. Also, comparing market prices will give you the legitimacy to negotiate the price of an item you covet and resell it at a higher price later on. Focus on niche items on which you can make the most profit. To be sure to be the first to see newly posted items, rely on Vinted bots.

Finally, keep in mind that a quality ad during the sale phase associated with the choice of the date and time of the sale is essential.

Appendix: Bots to boost your business

If you want to get serious about this buy and sell business, the use of a bot will be essential.

A Vinted bot is a robot that saves you time in searching for items to resell. Thanks to the speed of this tool, you can buy all the items you want faster than your competitors.

When a new ad is published on the site, the bot sends a notification as soon as possible. It is set to send only certain items based on your search. Once you receive the notification, all you have to do is click on the ad and buy the product if you are interested.

Among the many existing bots, I can recommend Distrobot, VintAlert, Vinz or Vinkit.

Distrobot

Distrobot is a bot designed to send you the latest items on sale on Vinted in a few seconds. This project was created more than a year ago by a team of experts, which is the origin of the concept of Vinted bots on Discord. Thanks to this bot, you will be able to buy all the items you want in a flash, so you can easily overtake your potential competitors.

This discord server also has a community space that is totally free. In addition to a freely accessible bot, you can chat with other members on a daily basis, which will make it easier for you to develop your knowledge in the field of buying and selling.

Distrobot offers from 10 to 50€/month.

VintAlert

VintAlert develops a mobile application that alerts you as soon as an item matching your search is published on Vinted. This robot monitors the searches registered on the Vinted marketplace and notifies you in real time by e-mail or mobile push. This way, you will be notified in advance when new articles are published on Vinted.

VintAlert offers a free daily alert system. Every day, you will receive an email with the new products available.

This bot helps you save money by buying items that are priced lower than their actual price.

Vinz

Vinz is a Chrome extension that you can install in your browser to do various things with your Vinted account. It saves time and allows you to do tasks that humans don't dare to do. Vinz works on computers and Android (mobile/tablet). Unfortunately, the Chrome extension is not yet available for iPhone/iPad. Also, Vinz can't work directly on their Vinted app. You have to go through their website.

This extension will allow you to repost Vinted's ads to highlight them in search results. This bot offers advanced filtering and sorting capabilities: you can sort by views, date, price or keyword.

Also, Vinz can add views to your listings and automatically send canned messages to Vinted who bookmark your items.

Vinz offers packages ranging from $6.99 to $34.99/month depending on the package you choose.

Vinkit

Vinkit is a Google Chrome extension that helps you make more sales and automatically republish your ads on Vinted in 2 clicks. Updating your ad will make it come up in search results when users sort items by "newest".

This extension also allows mass tracking. You can subscribe to thousands of user profiles and promote your profile. Also, some Vinties can follow you and increase your followers.

Vinkit offers one-month free trial. After that, the offers are 12€/month or 69€ for life.

Printed in Great Britain
by Amazon

32232526R00027